D0595437

Emergency Spanish

Ana Bremón

Series Editor: Jane Wightwick
Art Director: Mark Wightwick

Hippocrene Books, Inc.
New York

CONTENTS

Emergenc

Emergency

Spanish

CONTENTS

Spanish

⚡TAKE NOTE⚡

Traveling to a country where the language and culture are unfamiliar is exciting but can also be challenging. Often a smile and good manners will carry you a long way, and it helps to learn how to say at least "please" and "thank you."

When things are going smoothly on your trip you'll probably not notice the communication difficulties that can arise from a language barrier. Many people speak some English and will be happy to practice on you. But in more stressful situations, especially in remoter areas, you cannot always rely on English to make yourself understood or to get you out of a jam.

Emergency Spanish is designed for these situations. Carry it with you and use it to explain your situation clearly and to make polite requests. There's a pronunciation guide to help you say the words and phrases, or you can show the book to Spanish-speakers so that they can read it in their own language. There are even special "Point here" panels designed for them to point out an answer to your question.

So put **Emergency Spanish** in your pocket and travel light with confidence!

basics

KEY WORDS

yes	**sí** ◆ *see*
no	**no** ◆ *noh*
please	**por favor** ◆ *por fabor*
thank you	**gracias** ◆ *graseeas*
hello	**hola** ◆ *o-lah*
goodbye	**adiós** ◆ *addy-os*
where?	**¿dónde?** ◆ *dondeh*
here	**aquí** ◆ *ah-key*
when?	**¿cuándo?** ◆ *kwandoh*
now	**ahora** ◆ *ah-orah*
tomorrow	**mañana** ◆ *manyanah*
how much?	**¿cuánto?** ◆ *kwantoh*
I don't understand	**No entiendo** ◆ *noh entyendoh*

My name's…	**Me llamo…**
	◆ *meh yamoh*
What's your name?	**¿Cómo se llama?**
	◆ *komoh seh yamah*
Pleased to meet you	**Encantado**
	◆ *enkan-tadoh*
Where are you from?	**¿De dónde es?**
	◆ *deh dondeh es*
I'm American	**Soy americano (americana)**
	◆ *soy ah-mereekanoh* (fem: *ah-mereekanah*)
I'm English	**Soy inglés (inglesa)**
	◆ *soy eengles* (fem: *eenglesa*)

basics

I'm Canadian	**Soy canadiense** ◆ *soy kana-dyenseh*
I'm Irish	**Soy irlandés (irlandesa)** ◆ *soy eer-landes* (fem: *eer-landesah*)
I'm Scottish	**Soy escocés (escocesa)** ◆ *soy eskoses* (fem: *eskosesah*)
I'm Australian	**Soy australiano (australiana)** ◆ *soy owstra-leanoh* (fem: *owstra-leanah*)

please point here … muéstreme por favor …

Me llamo…	My name's…
Soy mexicano(-a)	I'm Mexican
Soy español(a)	I'm Spanish
Soy argentino(-a)	I'm Argentinian
Soy colombiano(-a)	I'm Colombian

muéstreme por favor … please point here …

basics

my husband	**mi marido** ◇ *mee mareedoh*
my wife	**mi mujer** ◇ *mee mooher*
my son	**mi hijo** ◇ *mee ee-hoh*
my daughter	**mi hija** ◇ *mee ee-hah*
my mother	**mi madre** ◇ *mee madreh*
my father	**mi padre** ◇ *mee padreh*
my sister	**mi hermana** ◇ *mee ermanah*
my brother	**mi hermano** ◇ *mee ermanoh*
my step-father	**mi padrastro** ◇ *mee padrastroh*
my step-mother	**mi madrastra** ◇ *mee madrastrah*
my step-daughter	**mi hijastra** ◇ *mee ee-hastrah*
my step-son	**mi hijastro** ◇ *mee ee-hastroh*

Down to

basics

This is my partner	**Ésta es mi pareja** ◇ *estah es mee pareh-hah*
I have two daughters	**Tengo dos hijas** ◇ *tengoh dos ee-has*
I have three sons	**Tengo tres hijos** ◇ *tengoh tres ee-hos*
My mother is here with us	**Mi madre está con nosotros** ◇ *mee madreh estah kon nosotros*

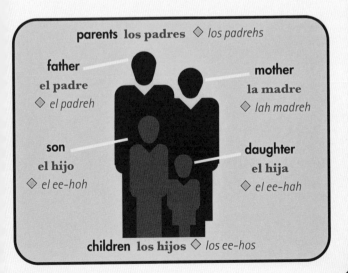

parents los padres ◇ *los padrehs*

father
el padre
◇ *el padreh*

mother
la madre
◇ *lah madreh*

son
el hijo
◇ *el ee-hoh*

daughter
el hija
◇ *el ee-hah*

children los hijos ◇ *los ee-hos*

KEY WORDS

bathroom	**el baño** ◆ *el banyoh*
bedroom	**el cuarto/dormitorio** ◆ *el kwartoh/dormee-toryo*
hot water	**el agua caliente** ◆ *el agwa kalyenteh*
toilet	**el excusado/retrete** ◆ *el eskoosadoh/retreteh*
sink	**el lavabo** ◆ *el lababoh*
faucet (tap)	**la llave/el grifo** ◆ *lah yabeh/el greefoh*
drain	**el desagüe** ◆ *el desagweh*
shower	**la regadera/ducha** ◆ *lah regaderah/doochah*
bathtub	**la tina/bañera** ◆ *lah teenah/banyerah*
soap	**el jabón** ◆ *el ha-bon*
towel	**la toalla** ◆ *lah toalya*
key	**la llave** ◆ *lah yabeh*

to stay

lock	**el cerrojo/pestillo** ◆ *el serrohoh/pesteeyoh*
door	**la puerta** ◆ *lah pwertah*
chair	**la silla** ◆ *lah seeyah*
table	**la mesa** ◆ *lah mesah*
television	**la televisión** ◆ *lah telebees-yon*
light	**la luz** ◆ *lah loos*
curtain	**la cortina** ◆ *lah korteenah*
bed	**la cama** ◆ *lah kamah*
blanket	**la cobija/manta** ◆ *lah kobeehah/mantah*
pillow	**la almohada** ◆ *lah almoh-adah*
heater	**el calentador** ◆ *el kalentador*
air-conditioning	**el aire acondicionado** ◆ *el ayreh akondeesyon-adoh*
crib (cot)	**la cuna** ◆ *lah koonah*

to stay

An extra towel, please	**Otra toalla, por favor** ◆ *otrah toalya por fabor*
May we have a crib (cot)?	**¿Tienen una cuna?** ◆ *tyenen oonah koonah*
May we have some soap?	**¿Tienen jabón?** ◆ *tyenen ha-bon*
The air-conditioning doesn't work	**El aire acondicionado no funciona** ◆ *el ayreh akondeesyon-adoh noh foonsyonah*
Please repair the heater	**¿Pueden arreglar el calentador?** ◆ *pweden ah-reglar el kalentador*
There's no hot water	**No hay agua caliente** ◆ *noh ay agwah kalyenteh*
It's too hot/cold	**Hace mucho calor/ frío** ◆ *aseh moochoh kalor/freeoh*
The light is broken	**La luz no funciona** ◆ *lah loos noh foonsyonah*

A place

to stay

The window is jammed	**La ventana no abre** ◇ *lah bentanah noh abreh*
I've lost my key	**He perdido la llave** ◇ *eh perdeedoh lah yabeh*
I can't open the door	**No puedo abrir la puerta** ◇ *noh pwedoh abreer lah pwertah*

please point here … muéstreme por favor …

Lo repararemos enseguida	We'll repair it right away
Voy a ayudarle	I'll come and help you
Se lo llevamos a la habitación	We'll bring it to your room
Pregúntele al conserje	Please ask the concierge
Pregunte en recepción	Please ask reception

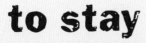
please point here … muéstreme por favor …

to stay

RENTING

kitchen	**la cocina** ◆ *lah koseenah*
living room	**la sala/el salón** ◆ *lah salah/el sa-lon*
dining room	**el comedor** ◆ *el komedor*
garbage	**la basura** ◆ *lah basoorah*
electric meter	**el medidor/contador** ◆ *el medeedor/kontador*
inventory	**el inventario** ◆ *el eenbentaryo*
Where do we pick up the keys?	**¿Dónde recogemos las llaves?** ◆ *dondeh rekoh-hemos las yabehs*

◢TAKE NOTE◣

When renting a summer vacation home, the most popular option is to take it for a full month or, if not, for a *quincenas* – the first and last 15 days of the month.

Where do we put the garbage?	**¿Dónde ponemos la basura?** ◆ *dondeh ponemos lah basoorah*
Are there any sheets/towels?	**¿Hay sábanas/toallas?** ◆ *ay sabanas/toalyas*
How much is the deposit?	**¿Cuánto es el depósito/ la fianza?** ◆ *kwantoh es el deposeetoh/lah fyansah*
Do we pay for cleaning?	**¿La limpieza se paga aparte?** ◆ *lah leemp-yesah seh pagah aparteh*

please point here … muéstreme por favor … please point here … muéstreme por favor … please point here …

Recoja las llaves en esta dirección	Pick up the keys at this address
Los esperaremos allí	We'll meet you there
Tiene que pagar eso aparte	You have to pay extra for that

PAYMENT

I need an invoice	**Necesito una factura** ◇ *neseseetoh oonah faktoorah*
The invoice has a mistake	**Esta factura tiene un error** ◇ *estah faktoorah tyeneh oon eh-ror*
We didn't have this	**Nosotros no pedimos esto** ◇ *nosohtros noh pedeemos estoh*
We only had one/two of these	**Nosotros sólo pedimos uno/dos de éstos** ◇ *nosotros soloh pedeemos oonoh/dos deh estos*
We didn't use the telephone	**Nosotros no usamos el teléfono** ◇ *nosotros noh oosamos el te-lefonoh*
We didn't break that	**Nosotros no rompimos eso** ◇ *nosotros noh rompeemos esoh*

to stay

We already paid for that	**Eso ya está pagado** ◆ *esoh yah estah pagadoh*
The manager, please	**El encargado, por favor** ◆ *el enkargadoh por fabor*
The total should be...	**El total debería ser...** ◆ *el total deberee-ah ser*

➡ **Page 74 for Numbers**

Voy a preguntar	Let me ask
Corregiremos eso	We'll correct that
La factura está correcta	The invoice is correct
Lo dedujimos del depósito/de la fianza	We deducted that from the deposit
Voy a avisar al encargado	I'll call the manager

to stay

KEY WORDS

map	**el mapa** ◆ *el mapah*
address	**la dirección** ◆ *lah deereks-yon*
street	**la calle** ◆ *lah kayeh*
highway	**la autopista** ◆ *lah awtopeestah*
distance	**la distancia** ◆ *lah deestanseeah*
meter	**el metro** ◆ *el metroh*
kilometer	**el kilómetro** ◆ *el keelometroh*
sign	**el letrero** ◆ *el letreroh*
direction	**la dirección** ◆ *lah deereks-yon*
right	**la derecha** ◆ *lah derechah*

we're lost!

left	**la izquierda** ◆ *lah eeskyerdah*
straight on	**todo derecho / recto** ◆ *todoh derechoh/rektoh*
junction	**el cruce** ◆ *el krooseh*
corner	**la esquina** ◆ *lah eskeenah*
traffic light	**el semáforo** ◆ *el semaforoh*
traffic circle (roundabout)	**la glorieta / rotonda** ◆ *lah gloreetah/rotondah*
on foot	**a pié / andando** ◆ *ah pee-eh/andandoh*
by car	**en coche** ◆ *en kocheh*
by bus	**en autobús** ◆ *en awtoboos*
by train	**en tren** ◆ *en tren*

Excuse me!	**¡Perdone!** ◆ *perdoneh*
Where's …?	**¿Dónde está…?** ◆ *dondeh estah*
What street is this?	**¿Cómo se llama esta calle?** ◆ *komoh seh yamah estah kayeh*
What building is this?	**¿Cómo se llama este edificio?** ◆ *komoh seh yamah esteh edeefeesyo*
Where are we on the map?	**¿Dónde estamos en la mapa/el plano?** ◆ *dondeh estamos en la mapah/el planoh*
Can you show me the way?	**¿Me puede decir cómo llegar?** ◆ *meh pwedeh deseer komoh yegar*
Is it far?	**¿Está lejos?** ◆ *estah leh-hos*

we're lost!

Le diré cómo llegar	I'll show you the way
Está cerca	It's close
Está lejos	It's far
Coja un autobús	Take a bus
Coja el metro	Take the subway (underground)
A la derecha	Right
A la izquierda	Left
La primera/ segunda/tercera calle	First/second/ third turn
Todo derecho/recto	Straight on
Cruce...	Cross ...
Pase...	Go past ...
Enfrente de	Opposite ...

➤ Page 24 for landmarks

I'm a visitor	**Estoy de visita** ◆ *estoy deh beeseetah*
I didn't know it was one-way	**No sabía que era de sentido único** ◆ *noh sabeeah keh erah deh senteedoh ooneekoh*
I can't read the sign	**No puedo leer el letrero** ◆ *noh pwedoh leh-er el letreroh*
How much is the fine?	**¿Cuánto es la multa?** ◆ *kwantoh es lah mooltah*

⚡TAKE NOTE⚡

If you drive your car into Mexico, make sure that you have insurance – available at border points. It's also a good idea to carry additional water and gasoline as distances between towns can be large.

In Spain, as well as ID, licence and insurance, the law requires drivers to carry a set of spare bulbs, a hazard triangle and a spare pair of prescription glasses if worn.

Excuse me,

we're lost!

TRAFFIC INSTRUCTIONS

no entry	**prohibido el paso** ◆ *proybeedoh el pasoh*
one-way	**sentido único** ◆ *senteedoh ooneekoh*
stop!	**¡pare!** ◆ *pareh*
slow down!	**¡baje su velocidad!** ◆ *baheh soo beloseedad*
keep right!	**¡manténgase a la derecha!** ◆ *manten-gaseh ah lah derechah*
keep left!	**¡manténgase a la izquierda!** ◆ *manten-gaseh ah lah eeskyerdah*
pedestrians only	**calle peatonal** ◆ *kayeh peahtonal*
buses only	**solo para autobuses** ◆ *soloh parah awtoboosehs*

we're lost!

LANDMARKS

airport	**el aeropuerto** ◆ *el aeropwertoh*
beach	**la playa** ◆ *lah ply-yah*
bridge	**el puente** ◆ *el pwenteh*
bus stop	**la parada de autobús** ◆ *lah paradah deh aootoboos*
campsite	**el cámping** ◆ *el kampeen*
castle	**el castillo** ◆ *el kasteeyoh*
cave	**la cueva** ◆ *lah kwebah*
church	**la iglesia** ◆ *lah eegleseeah*
ferry terminal	**la terminal del ferry** ◆ *lah termeenal del ferry*
forest	**el bosque** ◆ *el boskeh*
hostel	**el albergue** ◆ *el alberg-eh*
hotel	**el hotel** ◆ *el otel*

we're lost!

lake	**el lago** ◈ *el lagoh*
mountain	**la montaña** ◈ *lah montanyah*
movie theater (cinema)	**el cine** ◈ *el seeneh*
museum	**el museo** ◈ *el mooseh-oh*
park	**el parque** ◈ *el parkeh*
parking lot (car park)	**el estacionamiento / aparcamiento** ◈ *el estaseeonah-myentoh / aparkah-myentoh*
school	**el colegio** ◈ *el koleh-hyo*
square	**la plaza** ◈ *lah plasah*
station	**la estación** ◈ *lah estasyon*
tourist information	**la oficina de información** ◈ *lah ohfeeseenah deh eenformas-yon*
university	**la universidad** ◈ *lah ooneeberseedad*

KEY WORDS

appointment	**la cita** ◆ *lah seetah*
doctor	**el médico** ◆ *el medeekoh*
dentist	**el dentista** ◆ *el denteestah*
nurse	**la enfermera** ◆ *lah enfermerah*
ambulance	**la ambulancia** ◆ *lah amboo-lanseeah*
hospital	**el hospital** ◆ *el ospeetal*
clinic	**la clínica** ◆ *lah kleeneekah*
ward	**la planta** ◆ *lah plantah*
stretcher	**la camilla** ◆ *lah kameeyah*
injury	**la herida** ◆ *lah ereedah*
illness	**la enfermedad** ◆ *lah enfermedad*

doctor!

insurance	**el seguro** ◆ *el segooroh*
examination	**el examen** ◆ *el eksamen*
test	**la prueba** ◆ *lah prwebah*
prescription	**la receta** ◆ *lah resetah*
pharmacy	**la farmacia** ◆ *lah far-maseeah*
medicine	**la medicina** ◆ *lah medeeseenah*
pill	**la pastilla** ◆ *lah pasteeyah*
injection	**la inyección** ◆ *lah eenyeksyon*
syrup	**el jarabe** ◆ *el harabeh*
ointment	**la pomada** ◆ *lah pomadah*
suppository	**el supositorio** ◆ *el sooposee-toryo*
painkiller	**el analgésico** ◆ *el ahnal-heseekoh*

doctor!

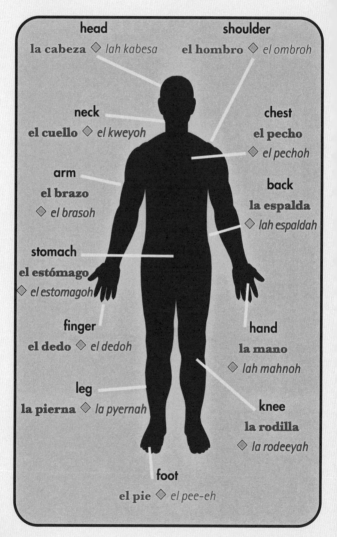

head
la cabeza ◇ *lah kabesa*

shoulder
el hombro ◇ *el ombroh*

neck
el cuello ◇ *el kweyoh*

chest
el pecho ◇ *el pechoh*

arm
el brazo ◇ *el brasoh*

back
la espalda ◇ *lah espaldah*

stomach
el estómago ◇ *el estomagoh*

finger
el dedo ◇ *el dedoh*

hand
la mano ◇ *lah mahnoh*

leg
la pierna ◇ *la pyernah*

knee
la rodilla ◇ *la rodeeyah*

foot
el pie ◇ *el pee-eh*

I need a

nose
la nariz ◇ *lah narees*

ear
la oreja ◇ *lah oreh-hah*

eye
el ojo ◇ *el oh-hoh*

cheek
la mejilla
◇ *lah meheeyah*

jaw
la mandíbula
◇ *lah mandeeboolah*

lip
el labio ◇ *la labyo*

mouth
la boca ◇ *lah bokah*

teeth
los dientes ◇ *los dyentes*

It hurts here	**Me duele aquí** ◆ *meh dweleh akee*
I can't move this	**No puedo mover esto** ◆ *noh pwedoh mober estoh*
I have a headache	**Me duele la cabeza** ◆ *meh dweleh lah kabesah*
I have a stomachache	**Me duele el estómago** ◆ *meh dweleh el estomagoh*
My back hurts	**Me duele la espalda** ◆ *meh dweleh lah espaldah*
I feel sick	**Voy a vomitar** ◆ *boy ah bohmeetar*
I have diarrhea	**Tengo diarrea** ◆ *tengoh deeareh-ah*

doctor!

Acuéstese aquí	Lie down here
Abra la boca	Open your mouth
Respire	Breathe deeply
Tosa	Cough
Súbase las mangas	Roll up your sleeves
Levante la camisa	Lift up your shirt

⚡TAKE NOTE⚡

Don't be alarmed if you are given an injection or suppositories when you are more used to taking tablets. Suppositories can be prescribed for anything from vitamins to painkillers and are a normal method of delivering medicine. Ask the doctor or chemist if there is a tablet alternative if you are unsure.

doctor!

I need a

Is it serious?
¿Es algo serio?
◆ *es algoh seryo*

Is it infectious?
¿Es contagioso?
◆ *es kontah-hyosoh*

Can it wait until I get home?
¿Puede esperar hasta que vuelva a casa?
◆ *pwedeh esperar astah keh bwelbah ah kasah*

Can you give me some painkillers?
¿Me puede dar algo para el dolor?
◆ *meh pwedeh dar algoh parah el dolor*

Where's the nearest pharmacy?
¿Dónde está la farmacia más cercana?
◆ *dondeh estah lah farmaseeah mas serkanah*

I need to contact my insurer
Tengo que hablar con mi seguro ◆ *tengoh keh ablar kon mee segooroh*

I'm not insured
No tengo seguro
◆ *noh tengoh segooroh*

I need a

doctor!

No es serio	It's not serious
Tiene una insolación	You have sunstroke
Tiene una infección	You have an infection
Todavía no estoy seguro	I'm not sure yet
Tengo que verlo otra vez	I need to see you again
Tiene que ir al hospital	You have to go to the hospital
No se asolee (ponga al sol)	Keep out of the sun
Beba mucha agua	Drink plenty of water
Tómese esta medicina	Take this medicine
¿Es usted alérgico a algo?	Are you allergic to anything?

doctor!

There's beer

KEY WORDS

car	**el coche** ◆ *el kocheh*
motorbike	**la moto** ◆ *lah motoh*
bicycle	**la bicicleta** ◆ *lah beeseekletah*
boat	**el barco** ◆ *el barkoh*
truck (lorry)	**el camión** ◆ *el kamyon*
tractor	**el tractor** ◆ *el traktor*
camper van	**el cámper/la roulotte** ◆ *el kampehr/lah roolot*
bus	**el autobús** ◆ *el awtoboos*
pedestrian	**el peatón** ◆ *el peh-aton*
child	**el niño** ◆ *el neenyoh*
dog	**el perro** ◆ *el perroh*
animal	**el animal** ◆ *el aneemal*

There's been

tree	**el árbol** ◆ *el arbol*
ditch	**la cuneta** ◆ *lah koonetah*
flood	**la inundación** ◆ *lah eenoon-dasyon*
cell phone (mobile phone)	**el celular/teléfono móvil** ◆ *el seloolar/telefonoh mobeel*
public telephone	**el teléfono público** ◆ *el telefonoh poobleekoh*
police	**la policía** ◆ *la poleeseeah*
ambulance	**la ambulancia** ◆ *lah amboo-lansya*
fire appliance	**el coche de bomberos** ◆ *el kocheh deh bomberos*
air and sea rescue	**el servicio de rescate por aire y mar** ◆ *el serbeesyo deh reskateh por ayreh ee mar*
witness	**el testigo** ◆ *el testeegoh*
insurance	**el seguro** ◆ *el segooroh*

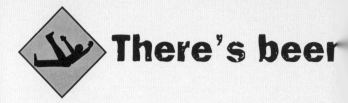

Please come quickly	**Dése prisa por favor** ◆ *deseh preesah por fabor*
Someone is hurt	**Hay alguien herido** ◆ *ay alghyen ereedoh*
Call an ambulance!	**¡Llame a una ambulancia!** ◆ *yameh ah oonah amboo-lansya*
Is there a telephone?	**¿Hay un teléfono?** ◆ *ay oon telefonoh*
Don't move him	**No lo mueva** ◆ *noh loh mwebah*
It wasn't our fault	**No fue culpa nuestra** ◆ *noh fwe koolpah nwestrah*
He/she saw it happen	**Él/Ella vió lo que pasó** ◆ *el/ehyah byo loh keh pasoh*

There's been

¿Dónde ocurrió?	Where did it happen?
¿Lo ha visto alguien?	Did anyone see it?
Tiene que denunciarlo	You need to report it
La licencia/El carnet, por favor	Your license, please
El seguro, por favor	Your insurance, please

⚡ TAKE NOTE ⚡

Watch out for speed bumps in many Mexican towns. They can be vicious if you drive over them too fast.

If an accident is not serious, both drivers usually sort it out on the spot. The police should be called if somebody is injured. Remember to carry your driving licence and insurance policy with you when driving.

trunk (boot)
la cajuela/el maletero
◇ *lah kahooehlah/maleteroh*

taillight
la luz trasera
◇ *lah loos traserah*

roof
el techo ◇ *el techoh*

exhaust
el tubo de escape
◇ *el tooboh deh eskapeh*

tire (tyre)
la llanta/el neumático
◇ *lah yantah/el neh-oomateekoh*

engine
el motor ◇ *el motor*

hood (bonnet)
el cofre / capó
◇ *el kofreh/kapoh*

headlight
la luz delantera
◇ *lah loos delanterah*

steering wheel
el volante
◇ *el bolanteh*

wheel
la rueda
◇ *lah rwedah*

fender (bumper)
la defensa / el parachoques
◇ *la defensah/el parachoh-kes*

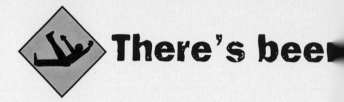
The hood is dented	**El cofre/capó está abollado** ◆ *el kofreh/kapoh estah aboyadoh*
The exhaust pipe fell off	**Se desprendió el tubo de escape** ◆ *seh desprendyo el tooboh deh eskapeh*
We have a flat (tire)	**Estamos ponchados/ Hemos pinchado** ◆ *estamos ponchados/ emos peenchadoh*
The engine won't start	**El motor no arranca** ◆ *el motor noh ah-rankah*
There's a hole in the boat	**El barco tiene un agujero** ◆ *el barkoh tyeneh oon agoo-hehroh*
There's something wrong with this	**A esto le pasa algo raro** ◆ *ah estoh leh pasah algoh raroh*
Can you repair it?	**¿Lo puede arreglar?** ◆ *loh pwedeh ah-reglar*

There's been

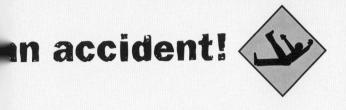
How long will it take?	¿Cuánto tiempo va a tardar? ◇ *kwantoh tyempoh bah ah tardar*
How much will it cost?	¿Cuánto costará? ◇ *kwantoh kostarah*

please point here … muéstreme por favor

Lo puedo reparar	I can repair it
Estará listo para hoy	It will be ready today
Estará listo para mañana	It will be ready tomorrow
Tengo que pedir la pieza	I have to order the part
No tiene arreglo	It can't be repaired
Le va a costar…	It will cost…

muéstreme por favor … please point here

KEY WORDS

account	**la cuenta** ◈ *lah kwentah*
ATM (cash machine)	**el cajero automático** ◈ *el kaheroh aooto-mateekoh*
bank	**el banco** ◈ *el bankoh*
bill (note)	**el billete** ◈ *el beeyeteh*
cash	**el contado / el dinero en metálico** ◈ *el kontadoh / el deeneroh en metaleekoh*
check (cheque)	**el cheque** ◈ *el chehkeh*
coin	**la moneda** ◈ *lah monedah*
commission	**la comisión** ◈ *lah komeesyon*
credit card	**la tarjeta de crédito** ◈ *lah tarhetah deh kredeetoh*
currency exchange	**el cambio de moneda** ◈ *el kambyo deh monedah*

talk

exchange rate	**el tipo de cambio** ◈ *el teepoh deh kambyo*
form	**la forma/el impreso** ◈ *la formah/el eempresoh*
ID	**la identificación** ◈ *lah eedenteefee-kasyon*
money	**el dinero** ◈ *el deeneroh*
pin number	**el nip/pin** ◈ *el neep/peen*
signature	**la firma** ◈ *lah feermah*
small change	**el cambio/la calderilla** ◈ *el kambeeyoh/ lah kaldereeyah*
teller (cashier)	**el cajero** ◈ *el kaheroh*
transfer	**la transferencia** ◈ *lah transferensya*
traveler's check (traveller's cheque)	**los cheques de viaje(ro)** ◈ *los chekes deh beea-heh(roh)*
withdrawal	**retirar dinero** ◈ *reteerar deeneroh*

talk

◄TAKE NOTE►

The currency in Latin America is mainly the *peso*, but the US dollar is also widely accepted. Spain is part of the Euro (€) zone. Be aware that in Spain banks usually close for siesta (1–2PM) and often do not reopen to the public.

Please change this into...	**Por favor, me cambia esto a...** ◆ *por fabor meh kambya estoh ah...*
What's the exchange rate?	**¿A cuánto está el cambio?** ◆ *ah kwantoh estah el kambyo*
I've forgotten my pin number	**Se me olvidó el nip/pin** ◆ *seh meh olbeedoh el neep/peen*
The ATM won't accept my card	**El cajero no acepta mi tarjeta** ◆ *el kaheroh noh aseptah mee tarhetah*
The ATM has swallowed my card	**El cajero se tragó mi tarjeta** ◆ *el kaheroh seh tragoh mee tarhetah*

I need to make a transfer	**Necesito hacer una transferencia**
	◆ *neseseetoh aser oonah transferensya*
How long will it take?	**¿Cuánto tardará?**
	◆ *kwantoh tardarah*

please point here … muéstreme por favor …

Enséñeme su pasaporte	Show me your passport
¿Cuál es su número de cuenta?	What's your account number?
Vaya a la caja	Go to the cashier
Éste no es el mismo nombre	This isn't the same name
Ésta no es la misma firma	This isn't the same signature

muéstreme por favor … please point here

SETTLING UP

check (bill)	**la cuenta** ◆ *lah kwentah*
service charge	**el servicio** ◆ *el serbeesyoh*
sales tax (VAT)	**el IVA** ◆ *el eebah*
cover charge	**el cubierto** ◆ *el koobyertoh*
tip	**la propina** ◆ *la propeenah*
receipt	**el recibo** ◆ *el reseeboh*
How much is this?	**¿Cuánto cuesta esto?** ◆ *kwanto kwestah estoh*
Is service included?	**¿Está incluido el servicio?** ◆ *estah inklueedoh el serbeesyoh*

Is tax included?	**¿Está incluido el impuesto?** ◇ *esta inklueedo el impwestoh*
A receipt, please	**Un recibo, por favor** ◇ *oon rehseeboh por fabor*

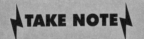

⚡TAKE NOTE⚡

Almost all large stores and most smaller ones now take credit cards. However, in some countries, notably Argentina, you could be faced with a hefty surcharge (*recargo*) as high as 5–10% of the purchase price.

The Spanish tax on goods is called IVA ("*eebah*") and it has different rates depending on the goods – up to 30% on some luxury goods. It is advisable to take your passport with you when shopping as foreign visitors can claim back the tax.

What's this amount for?	**¿De qué es esta cantidad?** ◆ *deh keh es estah kanteedad*
The total isn't right	**El total está incorrecto** ◆ *el total estah inkorrektoh*
That's too expensive	**Eso es demasiado caro** ◆ *esoh es demas-yadoh karoh*
I want to exchange this	**Quiero cambiar esto** ◆ *kyeroh kambyar estoh*
I want a refund	**Quiero que me devuelvan el dinero** ◆ *kyeroh keh meh debwelban el deeneroh*
I want to see the manager	**Quiero ver al encargado** ◆ *kyeroh ber al enkargadoh*

| I don't have another card | **No tengo otra tarjeta** ◆ *noh tengoh otrah tarhetah* |
| I've forgotten my wallet | **Se me olvidó la cartera** ◆ *seh olbeedoh lah karterah* |

please point here … muéstreme por favor …

No aceptamos tarjetas de crédito	We don't accept credit cards
No aceptamos esa tarjeta	We don't accept that card
Vaya a la caja	Go to the cashier
Le daré una factura detallada	I'll give you an itemised invoice

➡ Page 16–17 for hotel/accommodation

please point here … muéstreme por favor …

KEY WORDS

allergy	**la alergia** ◆ *lah ahheea*
calories	**las calorías** ◆ *las kaloreeas*
diabetic	**diabético** ◆ *dyabeteekoh*
diet	**la dieta** ◆ *lah dyetah*
fat	**la grasa** ◆ *lah grasah*
food poisoning	**la intoxicación alimenticia** ◆ *lah intokseekasyon aleeman-teeseeyah*
ingredients	**los ingredientes** ◆ *los ingredyentes*
intolerance	**la intolerancia** ◆ *lah intoleranseea*
salt	**la sal** ◆ *lah sal*
sugar	**el azúcar** ◆ *el asoocar*

vegetarian	**vegetariano**
	◆ *behetar-yanoh*
vegan	**ovolácteovegetariano**
	◆ *oboh-lakteoh-*
	behetar-yanoh

⚡TAKE NOTE⚡

Throughout the Spanish-speaking world, the main meal is generally lunch, served anywhere between one and four in the afternoon, with a lighter dinner at around nine in the evening. If eating out in a restaurant, expect to spend at least a couple of hours as service is unhurried.

Latin-American cuisine is largely based on corn and chili. But beyond that almost anything can be added to produce a fusion of tastes and colors. Spanish cuisine is also varied, with typical dishes changing from region to region. A popular snack food is *tapas*, an inexpensive way of trying a multitude of different dishes.

I'm allergic to...	**Soy alérgico a...** ◇ *soy alerheekoh ah...*
I don't eat...	**No como ...** ◇ *noh komoh...*
I don't like...	**No me gusta...** ◇ *noh meh goostah...*

➡ *Page 54–57 for types of food*

I'm vegetarian	**Soy vegetariano** ◇ *soy behetar-yanoh*
I'm diabetic	**Soy diabético** ◇ *soy dyabeteekoh*
Does this contain nuts?	**¿Contiene nueces?** ◇ *konteeyeneh nweses*
Does this contain wheat?	**¿Contiene trigo?** ◇ *konteeyeneh treegoh*
What meat is this?	**¿Qué carne es ésta?** ◇ *keh karneh es estah*

Are you sure?	¿Está usted seguro?
	◆ *estah oosted segooroh*
Can we check with the chef?	¿Podemos preguntarle al cocinero?
	◆ *podemos pregoon-tarleh al koseeneroh*

please point here … muéstreme por favor …

Lo podemos hacer sin ese ingrediente	We can make it without that ingedient
¿Por qué no prueba este platillo?	Why don't you try this dish?
Déjeme preguntarle el chef	Let me ask the chef
Lo siento, pero no tenemos nada adecuado	I'm sorry, we don't have anything suitable

muéstreme por favor … please point here …

FOOD FINDER

apple	**la manzana**	◆ *lah mansanah*
banana	**el plátano**	◆ *el platanoh*
beef	**la res/vaca**	◆ *lah res/bakah*
cabbage	**la col**	◆ *lah kol*
carrot	**la zanahoria**	◆ *lah sanahorya*
chicken	**el pollo**	◆ *el poyoh*
chili	**el chile/la guindilla** ◆ *el cheeleh/lah gheendeeyah*	
corn	**el maíz**	◆ *el mah-ees*
cucumber	**el pepino**	◆ *el pepeenoh*
duck	**el pato**	◆ *el patoh*
fish	**el pescado**	◆ *el peskadoh*
garlic	**el ajo**	◆ *el ah-hoh*
ginger	**el jengibre**	◆ *el henheebreh*
goat	**la cabra**	◆ *lah kabrah*
kidney	**el riñón**	◆ *el reenyon*
lamb	**el cordero**	◆ *el korderoh*
lemon	**el limón**	◆ *el leemon*
liver	**el hígado**	◆ *el eegadoh*
mushrooms	**los champiñones** ◆ *los champeenyoh-nes*	

I'm allergic

English–Spanish

nuts	**las nueces** ◇ *las nweses*
offal	**las asaduras** ◇ *las asadooras*
onion	**la cebolla** ◇ *lah seboyah*
orange	**la naranja** ◇ *lah naranhah*
peanuts	**los cacahuates** ◇ *los kaka-wates*
pigeon	**el pichón** ◇ *el peechon*
pork	**el cerdo** ◇ *el serdoh*
potato	**la papa/patata** ◇ *lah papah/patatah*
rabbit	**el conejo** ◇ *el konehoh*
shellfish	**el marisco** ◇ *el mareeskoh*
shrimp	**los camarones/las gambas** ◇ *los kamaronehs/las gambas*
soybeans	**las semillas de soya/soja** ◇ *las semeelyas deh soyah/sohah*
strawberries	**las fresas** ◇ *las fresas*
tomato	**el jitomate/tomate** ◇ *el heetomateh/tomateh*
veal	**la ternera** ◇ *lah ternerah*
venison	**el venado** ◇ *el benadoh*

FOOD FINDER

ajo	garlic
asaduras	offal
cabra	goat
cacahuates	peanuts
camarones	shrimp
cebolla	onion
cerdo	pork
champiñones	mushrooms
chile	chili
col	cabbage
conejo	rabbit
cordero	lamb
fresas	strawberries
gambas	shrimp
guindilla	chili
hígado	liver
jengibre	ginger
jitomate	tomato
limón	lemon
maíz	corn

to seafood!

Spanish–English

manzana	apple
marisco	shellfish
naranja	orange
nueces	nuts
papa/patata	potato
pato	duck
pepino	cucumber
pescado	fish
pichón	pigeon
plátano	banana
pollo	chicken
res	beef
riñón	kidney
semillas de soya/soja	soybeans
ternera	veal
tomate	tomato
vaca	beef
venado	venison
zanahoria	carrot

to seafood!

KEY WORDS

I've been robbed!	¡Me robaron! ◆ *meh robaron*
thief	el ladrón/robo ◆ *el ladron/roboh*
police	la policía ◆ *lah polee-seeyah*
police station	la delegación/comisaría ◆ *lah delegah-seeyon/ komeesah-reeyah*
report	la denuncia ◆ *lah denoonsya*
form	la forma/el impreso ◆ *lah formah/el eempresoh*
insurance	el seguro ◆ *el segooroh*
bag	la bolsa/el bolso ◆ *lah bolsah/ el bolsoh*
bracelet	la pulsera ◆ *lah poolserah*
briefcase	el portafolio/maletín ◆ *el portafolyoh/maleteen*

Stop,

camera	**la cámara** ◆ *lah kamarah*
car	**el coche** ◆ *el kocheh*
cell phone (mobile phone)	**el celular/teléfono móvil** ◆ *el seloolar/ telefonoh mobeel*
computer	**la computadora/ el ordenador** ◆ *lah kompootadorah/ el ordenador*
credit card	**la tarjeta de crédito** ◆ *lah tarhetah deh kredeetoh*
earrings	**los aretes/pendientes** ◆ *los aratehs/pendyentes*
money	**el dinero** ◆ *el deeneroh*
necklace	**el collar** ◆ *el koyar*
passport	**el pasaporte** ◆ *el pasaporteh*
wallet	**la cartera** ◆ *lah karterah*
watch	**el reloj** ◆ *el relogh*

thief!

| I want to report a theft | **Quiero denunciar un robo** ◆ *kyeroh denoonsyar oon roboh* |

I've lost... **Perdí/He perdido...** ◆ *perdee/eh perdeedoh*

I was mugged **Me asaltaron** ◆ *meh asaltaron*

It was taken from my bag **Me lo robaron de la bolsa** ◆ *meh loh robaron deh lah bolsah*

It was taken from my pocket **Me lo robaron del bolsillo** ◆ *meh loh robaron del bolseeyoh*

It was taken from my hotel room **Me lo robaron de la habitación del hotel** ◆ *meh loh robaron deh lah abeetas-yon del ohtel*

It happened today **Fue hoy** ◆ *fweh oy*

It happened yesterday	**Fue ayer**
	◆ *fweh ah-yer*
I need a report for my insurance	**Necesito la denuncia para el seguro**
	◆ *neseseetoh lah denoonsya parah el segooroh*

⚡TAKE NOTE⚡

There is no doubt that while traveling in some parts of Latin America you should be very vigilant to avoid becoming a victim of theft.

The most common form of theft is small-scale pick-pocketing, particularly in stations and other crowded places. You should be careful to keep money and valuables out of reach and sight as much as possible. Make use of hotel safes if these are available.

When reporting a theft you need to go in person to the nearest police station. Once there, you will be given a copy of the report for you to keep. Passports need to be reported at the nearest consulate as well, where they will be dealing with a replacement. Stolen credit cards should also be reported to the issuing companies and rental cars to the rental company as soon as possible.

DESCRIBING ITEMS

new	**nuevo** ◆ *nweboh*
old	**viejo** ◆ *byehoh*
big	**grande** ◆ *grandeh*
small	**pequeño** ◆ *pekenyoh*
black	**negro** ◆ *negroh*
blue	**azul** ◆ *asool*
brown	**café/marrón** ◆ *kafeh/mar-ron*
green	**verde** ◆ *berdeh*
orange	**naranja** ◆ *naranhah*
pink	**rosa** ◆ *rosah*
purple	**morado** ◆ *moradoh*
red	**rojo** ◆ *roh-hoh*
white	**blanco** ◆ *blankoh*
yellow	**amarillo** ◆ *amareeyoh*

silver	**plateado** ◆ *plateh-adoh*
gold	**dorado** ◆ *doradoh*
leather	**de cuero** ◆ *deh kweroh*
valuable	**valioso** ◆ *balyosoh*

please point here ... muéstreme por favor ...

¿Qué falta?	What's missing?
¿De qué color era?	What color was it?
¿Cuál era su valor?	How much was it worth?
¿Tenía su nombre en algún sitio?	Did it have your name on it?

muéstreme por favor ... please point here

DESCRIBING PEOPLE

man	woman
el hombre ◇ *el ombreh*	**la mujer** ◇ *lah mooher*

glasses los anteojos/las gafas
◇ *los anteh-ohos/las gafas*

short hair
el pelo corto
◇ *el peloh kortoh*

long hair
el pelo largo
◇ *el peloh largoh*

moustache
el bigote
◇ *el beegoteh*

beard
la barba
◇ *lah barbah*

about ... years old   **de unos ... años**
◇ *deh oonos ... anyos*

tall	**alto** ◇ *altoh*
short	**bajo** ◇ *bah-hoh*
fat	**gordo** ◇ *gordoh*
thin	**delgado** ◇ *delgadoh*
old	**viejo** ◇ *byehoh*
young	**joven** ◇ *hohben*

please point here ... muéstreme por favor ...

Por favor rellene esta forma	Please fill out this form
Firme aquí	Sign here
Nos encargaremos de esto	We'll look into it
Hemos encontrado el artículo	We've found the item
Voy a buscar a alguien que hable inglés	I'll find someone who speaks English

muéstreme por favor ... please point here

KEY WORDS

arrest	**el arresto** ◆ *el arrestoh*
attorney (lawyer)	**el abogado** ◆ *el abogadoh*
bail	**la fianza** ◆ *lah fyanzah*
charge	**el cargo** ◆ *el kargoh*
consulate	**el consulado** ◆ *el konsooladoh*
court	**el juzgado** ◆ *el hoosgadoh*
defense	**la defensa** ◆ *lah defensah*
deportation	**la deportación** ◆ *lah deportas-yon*
embassy	**la embajada** ◆ *lah embah-hadah*
fine	**la multa** ◆ *lah mooltah*

interpreter	**el intérprete** ◆ *el eenterpreteh*
judge	**el juez** ◆ *el hwes*
law	**la ley** ◆ *lah ley*
police	**la policía** ◆ *lah poleesee-ah*
police officer	**el agente de policía** ◆ *el ahenteh deh poleesee-ah*
police station	**la delegación / comisaría** ◆ *lah delegah-seeyon/ komeesah-reeyah*
prison	**la cárcel** ◆ *lah karsel*
prosecution	**el procesamiento** ◆ *el prosesa-myentoh*
statement	**la declaración** ◆ *lah deklaras-yon*
suspect	**el sospechoso** ◆ *el sospechosoh*
warning	**la advertencia** ◆ *lah adbertensya*

Keeping ou

⚡TAKE NOTE⚡

When you are outside your hotel you should always have your passport or other form of identification on you. If you are approached by anyone claiming to be a plain-clothes police officer, you should ask to see *their* ID and insist on going to the nearest police station. Impersonating an officer is a scam used in some parts of Latin America to extract "fines" from tourists.

I apologise	**Lo siento mucho** ◆ *loh syentoh moochoh*
I'm just visiting	**Sólo estoy de paso** ◆ *soloh estoy deh pasoh*
It wasn't me	**No fui yo** ◆ *noh fwee yoh*
I don't understand	**No entiendo** ◆ *noh entyendoh*
I can't read the sign	**No puedo leer el letrero** ◆ *noh pwedoh leher el letreroh*

Keeping out

I didn't know it wasn't allowed	**No sabía que no estaba permitido**
	◆ *noh sabee-ah keh noh estabah permee-teedoh*
Am I under arrest?	**¿Estoy detenido?**
	◆ *estoy deteneedoh*

please point here … muéstreme por favor …

Eso es ilegal	That's illegal
Esta vez queda usted advertido	I'll just warn you this time
Tiene que pagar una multa	You have to pay a fine
Por favor enséñeme su pasaporte	Please show me your passport
Tiene que acompañarnos a la delegación	You need to come to the station

muéstreme por favor … please point here …

Can I call the American embassy?	**¿Puedo llamar a la embajada americana?** ◆ *pwedoh yamar ah lah embahadah amereekanah*
Can I call the British embassy?	**¿Puedo llamar a la embajada británica?** ◆ *pwedoh yamar ah lah embahadah breetaneekah*
Can I call the Canadian consulate?	**¿Puedo llamar al consulado canadiense?** ◆ *pwedoh yamar al konsooladoh kanadyenseh*
I need an English-speaking lawyer	**Necesito un abogado que hable inglés** ◆ *neseseetoh oon abogadoh keh ableh eengles*
I need to contact my family	**Necesito hablar con mi familia** ◆ *neseseetoh ablar kon mee fameelya*

| I don't know anything about it | **Yo no sé nada de eso** ◆ *yoh noh seh nadah deh esoh* |
| I can't say anything yet | **Todavía no puedo decir nada** ◆ *todabee-ah noh pwedo deseer nadah* |

please point here ... muéstreme por favor ...

¿Quiere hacer una declaración?	Do you want to make a statement?
¿Quiere hacer una llamada?	Do you want to make a phone call?
Éstos son sus derechos	These are your rights
Voy a traer a un intérprete	I'm bringing an interpreter
Su familia está aquí	Your family is here

muéstreme por favor ... please point here ...

Keeping ou

⚡TAKE NOTE⚡

Keeping out of trouble with the law is generally only a matter of common sense. What is illegal at home is probably also illegal on vacation! However, be particularly careful to avoid approaching or photographing military insallations or personnel.

Both in Latin America and in Spain you will find police officers who speak English in the cities and main tourist resorts. But in the smaller towns and villages, you may need to communicate at some point in Spanish – with the help of this phrasebook!

What are you charging me with?	**¿De qué se me acusa?** ◆ *deh keh seh meh akoosah*
How much is the fine?	**¿Cuánto es la multa?** ◆ *kwantoh es lah mooltah*
Can I post bail?	**¿Puedo pagar la fianza?** ◆ *pwedoh pagar lah fyansah*

# of trouble

Will I have to go to court?	¿Tengo que ir a juicio?
	◆ *tengoh keh eer ah huysyo*
How long do I have to stay here?	¿Cuánto tiempo tengo que quedarme?
	◆ *kwantoh tyempoh tengoh keh kedarmeh*

please point here ... muéstreme por favor ...

No le vamos a levantar un cargo	We won't be charging you
Puede marcharse	You're free to go
Tiene que volver	You need to come back
Por favor deje su pasaporte	Please leave your passport
Tiene que contestar unas preguntas	You'll need to answer some questions

muéstreme por favor ... please point here ...

NUMBERS

one	**uno** ◆ *oono*
two	**dos** ◆ *dos*
three	**tres** ◆ *tres*
four	**cuatro** ◆ *kwatroh*
five	**cinco** ◆ *seenkoh*
six	**seis** ◆ *seys*
seven	**siete** ◆ *syeteh*
eight	**ocho** ◆ *ochoh*
nine	**nueve** ◆ *nwebeh*
ten	**diez** ◆ *dyes*
eleven	**once** ◆ *onseh*
twelve	**doce** ◆ *doseh*
thirteen	**trece** ◆ *treseh*
fourteen	**catorce** ◆ *katorseh*
fifteen	**quince** ◆ *keenseh*
sixteen	**dieciséis** ◆ *dyesee-seys*
seventeen	**diecisiete** ◆ *dyesee-syeteh*
eighteen	**dieciocho** ◆ *dyesee-ochoh*
nineteen	**diecinueve** ◆ *dyesee-nwebeh*

twenty	**veinte** ◆ *beynteh*
twenty-one	**veintiuno** ◆ *veyntee-oonoh*
twenty-two	**veintidós** ◆ *veyntee-dos*
thirty	**treinta** ◆ *treyntah*
forty	**cuarenta** ◆ *kwarentah*
fifty	**cincuenta** ◆ *seenkwentah*
sixty	**sesentah** ◆ *sesentah*
seventy	**setenta** ◆ *setentah*
eighty	**ochenta** ◆ *ochentah*
ninety	**noventa** ◆ *nobentah*
hundred	**cien** ◆ *syen*
thousand	**mil** ◆ *meel*

⚡TAKE NOTE⚡

For Spanish dates you can use ordinary numbers rather than cardinal ones (1st, 2nd, etc.), e.g. *diez de octubre* = 10th of October. Years have to be read as a number, using thousands, e.g. 1960 = *mil novecientos sesenta* ("one thousand nine hundred sixty").

In Spain decimal numbers are separated by a comma, e.g. 25,49. But in Latin America a period (full stop) is used as in English, e.g. 25.49.

What's the time?

¿Qué hora es?
◆ *keh orah es*

It's two o'clock

Son las dos
◆ *son las dos*

las once
◆ *las onseh*

11:15

las once y cuarto
◆ *las onseh ee kwartoh*

14:30

las dos y media
◆ *las dos ee medya*

14:45

**cuarto para las tres/
las tres menos cuarto**
◆ *kwartoh parah las tres/
las tres menos kwartoh*

Monday	**lunes** ◈ *loones*
Tuesday	**martes** ◈ *martes*
Wednesday	**miércoles** ◈ *mee-erloles*
Thursday	**jueves** ◈ *hwebes*
Friday	**viernes** ◈ *byernes*
Saturday	**sábado** ◈ *sabadoh*
Sunday	**domingo** ◈ *domeengoh*
now	**ahora** ◈ *ah-orah*
soon	**pronto** ◈ *prontoh*
today	**hoy** ◈ *oy*
yesterday	**ayer** ◈ *ah-yer*
tomorrow	**mañana** ◈ *manyanah*

MONTHS

January	**enero** ◆ *eneroh*	
February	**febrero** ◆ *febreroh*	
March	**marzo** ◆ *marsoh*	
April	**abril** ◆ *abreel*	
May	**mayo** ◆ *mah-yoh*	
June	**junio** ◆ *hoonyo*	
July	**julio** ◆ *hoolyo*	
August	**agosto** ◆ *ahgostoh*	
September	**septiembre** ◆ *septyembreh*	
October	**octubre** ◆ *oktoobreh*	
November	**noviembre** ◆ *nobyembreh*	
December	**diciembre** ◆ *deesyembreh*	
What's the date?	**¿Qué fecha es?** ◆ *keh fechah es*	
It's June 12	**Es el doce de junio** ◆ *es el doseh deh hoonyo*	

?

SIGNS

ENTRANCE
ENTRADA

EXIT
SALIDA

RESTROOMS
SERVICIOS/
BAÑOS

MEN
CABALLEROS

WOMEN
SEÑORAS/
DAMAS

SLOW
DESPACIO

NO ENTRY
PROHIBIDA LA
ENTRADA

DANGER
PELIGRO

NO SMOKING
PROHIBIDO
FUMAR

Copyright © 2003 g-and-w PUBLISHING

ISBN 0-7818-0977-0

For information, address:
Hippocrene Books, Inc.
171 Madison Avenue
New York, NY 10016

Cataloging-in-Publication data available from the Library of Congress

Developed by g-and-w PUBLISHING, Oxfordshire, UK
www.g-and-w.co.uk
Designed by Upfront Creative, London, UK
www.upfrontcreative.com

Printed in China

03 04 05 06 07 08   12 11 10 9 8 7 6 5 4 3 2 1